Meet

George Washington

Meet

George Washington

by Patricia A. Pingry

Illustrated by Stephanie McFetridge Britt

ideals children's books™

Nashville, Tennessee

ISBN 0-8249-4131-4

Published by Ideals Children's Books
An imprint of Ideals Publications
A division of Guideposts
535 Metroplex Drive, Suite 250
Nashville, Tennessee 37211

Printed and bound in Mexico by RR Donnelley & Sons

Color scans by Precision Color Graphics, Franklin, WI

Library of Congress Cataloging-in-Publication Data

Pingry, Patricia.
   Meet George Washington / by Patricia A. Pingry ; illustrated by
Stephanie McFetridge Britt.
      p. cm.
Summary: A biography of the nation's first president, including his
youth in Virginia, his army career, and his leadership of the newly
formed United States of America.
   ISBN 0-8249-4131-4 (alk. paper)

 1. Washington, George, 1732-1799--Juvenile literature. 2. Presidents--
United States--Biography--Juvenile literature. [1. Washington, George,
1732-1799. 2. Presidents.] I. Britt, Stephanie, ill. II. Title.
   E312.66.P55 2001
    973.4'1'092--dc21
                                 2001005818

10 8 6 4 2 1 3 5 7 9

Designed by Eve DeGrie

*Thank you to Dorothy Twohig, Editor-in-Chief Emeritus,
The Papers of George Washington, University of Virginia,
for reading this manuscript and offering her comments.*

For Brandon

" . . . first in war,
first in peace,
and first in the hearts
of his countrymen."
—Henry Lee

"George, Betty, Jack, Samuel," called Gus Washington. **"Your brother Lawrence is here."**

The brothers raced with their sister through the fields of Ferry Farm with eight-year-old George leading the way. George was always so excited when his half brother Lawrence came to visit.

"Now George, be careful," called his mother, Mary Ball Washington.

"Don't run through the house.

Please sit down and rest."

But George did not sit down. His mother was always fussing over him. George thought it was because his mother was almost struck by lightning shortly before his birth on February 22, 1732. Mary Ball had been so frightened that she never wanted George to do anything that could possibly harm him. But George thought that, because the lightning bolt had missed, nothing could ever hurt him.

George was adventurous. He liked to go hunting with his

father. He loved to ride his pony through the fields. He helped

his father with the farmwork.

George ran into the parlor. He stopped and stared. Lawrence was wearing an army uniform of blue pants and red jacket. A silver sword sparkled at his side.

"**Lawrence,**" George exclaimed, "**you're in the army!**"

Right then and there, George vowed that someday he would become a military officer, not just a country farmer from the colony of Virginia. He wanted to be a British officer, just like Lawrence. His mother couldn't tell him to stop running through the house then!

The next morning, George got up very early and walked down to the Rappahannock River. He leaped onto the ferry, just like every morning, and rode across the river to Fredericksburg.

A few blocks up the road was the tiny school-house where George learned reading and arithmetic. To practice writing, he copied the *Rules of Civility and Decent Behaviour in Company and Conversation* in his notebook.

After school, George walked back to the ferry and rode home.

When George was eleven, his father died. His mother allowed him to visit often with Lawrence at his home, Mount Vernon. George studied to learn what a military officer would need to know: geometry, trigonometry, and even surveying. There were parties too. George learned to dance, and he remembered the *Rules of Civility*. Someday he wanted to be a polite military officer.

George grew strong and tall. At sixteen, he was six feet, two inches tall. He was hired by one of Virginia's largest landowners to survey land in the Shenandoah Valley. In the valley, George camped out, met with Native Americans and learned that he could take care of himself.

When George was twenty-one, he joined the army and commanded Virginia's troops in the French and Indian War until 1758. George learned how to lead an army. When the war was over, George wanted to go home to Mount Vernon.

George's beloved brother Lawrence had died and left Mount Vernon to George. George studied books on farming. He read about planting. He rotated his crops.

George had slaves who worked on his plantation. Although he did not break up families as other plantation owners did, he began to think that perhaps no one should own another person.

One day in 1758, George visited a beautiful young widow, Martha Custis, and her two children. George enjoyed his visit so much that he went back the next day. Soon, he asked Martha to be his wife.

George was a wonderful stepfather. He ordered dolls from England for Patsy, his new stepdaughter. He ordered toy soldiers for Jacky, his new stepson.

George became a member of Virginia's government. He went to Williamsburg to make the laws. Then he went back home to Mount Vernon. George and Martha, Patsy and Jacky were very happy.

But Britain needed money. They began to tax the colonies. To pay the tax, many colonists would have to sell some of their land. George became angry. It was not fair to make the colonies send money to England.

Other men were angry too. On July 4, 1776, the Continental Congress signed a Declaration of Independence. George knew this meant war with the British.

Congress named George commander in chief of the army. This was his childhood dream. He was a general. He would lead an army. But what an army it was.

George had a uniform, but his men did not. They did not have enough guns or bullets. They needed more blankets and tents. But worst of all, the men from New York, Massachusetts, and New Jersey didn't like the general from Virginia. And the men from Virginia didn't want to fight with men from New York or North Carolina.

George politely wrote Congress for guns and uniforms. Then he set about to pull his troops together.

On Christmas night in 1776, George's men were freezing. Their shoes were worn out. Some wrapped rags around their feet. It was snowing and sleeting. George stopped his horse on the banks of the Delaware River and saw large ice blocks floating down the river. He knew that the British were just across the river in New Jersey. George also knew that in six days, most of his men's army time would be up and they would go home. George needed a victory now, or the war would be lost.

"We cross the river tonight," he said. He sent orders to his generals to bring their men across too.

But George's generals looked at the river and the snow and the ice. They said, **"No one can cross the river. We might drown. We won't even try."** They went back to their tents.

George Washington led his men into boats and across the river to Trenton, New Jersey. He won a victory.

George led his army in battle for six more years. In 1781, at

Yorktown, Virginia, the British surrendered. The Americans

thought that George was the greatest general ever.

The American Revolution was over, but America needed a better government. In 1787, the Constitutional Convention met in Philadelphia. Everyone at the convention knew that George would be the first president.

But George was not sure that he wanted to be president. He was respected as the leader of the army. If he became president, the people might not love him. But George could not refuse to serve his country one more time.

In 1789, George was elected the first president of the United States.

George served as president for eight years.

Then he said, **"I'm tired. I want to go home."**

George and Martha left for Mount Vernon. A crowd of people lined the road to see Washington. They shouted, **"Thanks, George."** They yelled, **"We'll miss you!"** George knew that he still had the people's respect and love.

At Mount Vernon, George read books on farming. He wrote letters, planted seeds, and harvested crops. Many Americans came to see him. He and Martha always had company for dinner.

George still had slaves who worked on his farms, but he knew that slavery was wrong. After all, he fought a war because he believed that **"all men are created equal."** When Washington died in 1799, his will freed his slaves.

After George's death, the new capital of the United States was completed. It was named Washington, D.C., in honor of George.

Then the people built a tall monument to honor him. They put a picture of his face on the one-dollar bill and the quarter.

As a child, George had been so impressed by his brother's uniform that he wanted the respect the uniform demanded. He grew up to become a great general and the first president of the United States. George gained the respect of the world, but not because of the uniform. We respect George because he was brave, smart, honorable, kind, and . . .

always polite.